Praise for

365 Daily Affirmations for Friendship

"Jan Yager knows friendship and helps us value it more and enjoy it to the fullest with her wonderful book of powerful and positive affirmations. They'll help you be a better friend to everyone in your world and to yourself."

—Victoria Moran, author of *Creating a Charmed Life*

"In *365 Daily Affirmations for Friendship*, Dr. Jan Yager sheds a light on friendship, a wonderfully complex, multi-layered, beneficial, fun, yet often challenging subject, with insights that I hadn't known or ever considered. Her daily affirmations are enlightening and truly inspiring!"

—Mary Jones, talk show host

"Jan Yager's book, *365 Daily Affirmations for Friendship*, is intelligent, insightful and open-hearted, guaranteed to have you smiling in appreciation for yourself and your friends."

—Stephanie Dale, author of *My Pilgrim's Heart*

"*365 Daily Affirmations for Friendship* offers fresh friendship insights in its interesting introduction and inspiring affirmations, a recommended addition to your library of friendship books to be read and referred to again and again."

—Charlotte Libov, award-winning health writer

"Friendship is true love toward another human being. In her new book, *365 Daily Affirmations for Friendship*, Dr. Yager shows you how to get the most from your friendships."

—Beverly Solomon,
creative director for artist Pablo Solomon

365 DAILY AFFIRMATIONS
For Friendship

Selected Other Books by Jan Yager, Ph.D.

Nonfiction

365 Daily Affirmations for Happiness
365 Daily Affirmations for Time Management
365 Daily Affirmations for Creative Weight Management
When Friendship Hurts
Friendshifts®
125 Ways to Meet the Love of Your Life
Single in America
Road Signs on Life's Journey
Productive Relationships
Who's That Sitting at My Desk?
Grow Global
Business Protocol
Effective Business and Nonfiction Writing
Work Less, Do More
Creative Time Management for the New Millennium
Creative Time Management
Career Opportunities in the Film Industry (with Fred Yager)
Career Opportunities in the Publishing Industry
(with Fred Yager)
Victims
The Help Book

Fiction

The Pretty One
Untimely Death (with Fred Yager)
Just Your Everyday People (with Fred Yager)
The Cantaloupe Cat (illustrated by Mitzi Lyman)
The Healing Power of Mourning: Poems (anthology)

365 DAILY AFFIRMATIONS
For Friendship

Jan Yager, Ph.D.

HANNACROIX CREEK BOOKS, INC.
Stamford, Connecticut

This book is dedicated to my husband Fred, our sons Scott and Jeff, our grandson Bradley, Nicole, my sister Eileen, my Mom, my extended family, and my friends

Copyright © 2012 by Jan Yager, Ph.D.

Cover design by Scribe Freelance | www.scribefreelance.com

Published by:
Hannacroix Creek Books, Inc.
1127 High Ridge Road, #110
Stamford, Connecticut 06905 USA
http://www.hannacroixcreekbooks.com
e-mail: hannacroix@aol.com
Follow us on twitter: www.twitter.com/hannacroixcreek

ISBN: 1-889262-72-2 (trade paperback)
    978-1-889262-72-7

Library of Congress Cataloging-in-Publication Data

Yager, Jan, 1948-
  365 daily affirmations for friendship / Jan Yager.
    p. cm.
  ISBN 978-1-889262-72-7
1. Friendship. I. Title. II. Title: Three hundred sixty five daily affirmations for friendship.
  BF575.F66Y3394 2012
  177'.62--dc23
                                2012001035

Contents

A Look at Friendship	1
PART 1	37
Affirmations 1-365	39
Write your own affirmations	134
PART 2: Friendship Activities	137
At Work	139
At Leisure	143
Bibliography	149
Resources	157
About the Author	159

DISCLAIMER

The purpose of this book is to provide inspiration, opinions, and information on the topics covered. It is sold with the understanding that the publisher and author are *not* engaged in rendering psychological or other professional services. This book is *not* intended to be used as a substitute for psychological support or therapy if professional help is needed.

Typographical or content mistakes may inadvertently be contained in this book. In addition, information may not apply to everyone; it might also be out of date especially because new findings may have been unavailable until after the date of this book's completion, printing, or distribution.

This book is intended for people who have essentially healthy attitudes toward friendship and relationships. The author and the publisher have neither liability nor responsibility to any person or entity in regard to any loss or damage caused, or alleged to be caused, directly or indirectly by the opinions or information contained in this book.

Self-help groups, associations, or other resources related to friendship may be mentioned in this book but inclusion does not indicate endorsement nor does exclusion imply anything negative about services, associations, or products that are not included.

You may put a great deal of time and effort into reading this book and in completing one or all of the activities in it. However, you still may not get the results that you wish. Neither the publisher nor the author in any way promise friendship, career, or lifestyle success or happiness.

A Look at Friendship

When Laura Crawley and Stephanie Kandrac began kindergarten at the age of five back in 1985, it was also the start of a lifelong best friendship. Twenty years later, when Laura was hospitalized with a brain tumor, Stephanie would visit her frequently. She became the central communicator, with updates to their friends about Laura's condition as well as ways they could help.

As the number of people who wanted to lend a hand kept growing, Stephanie, her sister, Aimee, and their mother, Fran, turned to technology by creating a simple website to provide a more systematic way of coordinating their "team approach" to helping a friend through a crisis.

For Laura, her team provided everything from e-mail communications about how she was doing to sending a chorus of friends and friends of friends — 60 in all —to sing Christmas carols outside Laura's house to cheer her up when she was too sick to leave her home.

By the time Laura passed away in August of 2006, eleven months after her diagnosis, her team had grown to over 200. This friends-helping-friends movement is a legacy to Laura, even if she did not get to see the launch ten months later, in June of 2007, of the site http://whatfriendsdo.com.

Over the next few years, the free site has expanded to the point that it now has thousands of friend teams using it to organize their helping efforts. Friends sign up to coordinate assistance and sharing information for everything from having a baby to dealing with a health challenge or the death of a loved one.

What is a friend?

Laura and Stephanie were friends in the truest sense of the word. In addition to keeping their friendship going throughout their childhood, teen, and early young adult years, even though they attended different high schools and colleges, Stephanie came through for Laura when she needed her the most, at the time of a dire health crisis.

Friend. A word that evokes wonderful feelings in those who have been blessed with positive and caring close or best friends, who, like Stephanie, have been there for them when times were tough and when times were joyful.

But the word *friend* can also stir up a sense of frustration and pain in those who have been hurt by someone to whom they felt a bond, who have never had a close friend, or who have lost a friend because of drifting apart, disagreement, or the unresolved grief and sense of loss that they feel because their friend has passed away.

The ancient philosopher Aristotle considered a true friend "another self." Philosopher Cicero wrote: "What could be finer than to have someone to whom you may speak as freely as to yourself?" Sixteenth century English philosopher Francis Bacon similarly considered a friend "another himself." French essayist Montaigne saw a friend as a "second self." Actress Marlene Dietrich is quoted as saying, "It's the friends you can call up at 4 a.m. that matter."

Categories of friends

In my doctoral dissertation on friendship, I found it necessary to divide friendship into three distinct types, and to define each one: best, close, or casual friends. While all three categories are friends, each has a key difference in its degree of intimacy, as well as what level of confidences are shared, from little to none for casual friends to some or all for close or best friends depending on each friend's personality and tolerance for self-disclosure.

Close or best friends are similar; the main difference is that there is usually only one or two best friends; the number of close friends is usually greater— four to six— as the relationship is usually less demanding of one's time or exclusivity then a best friend and therefore easier to maintain with more people.

Close or best friends are those with whom you feel you can say anything you want, *but*—and this is a big and an important *but*—*you* decide *if* you want to say it. Yes, that friend would be open to hearing your opinion on anything or anyone, but you have to be careful.

Casual friends are more than an acquaintance but what is shared tends to be more informational and less revealing than what is entrusted to a close or best friend. However, there is what I call the "cab driver self-disclosure phenomenon," whereby someone will share on the deepest level with a total stranger about feelings or experiences that they may not share with a casual friend or even a close or best friend. It is the anonymity of the cab driver that for some makes the self-disclosure easier.

There are common traits to all three categories of relationships we call a *friend*. A friend is someone who has chosen to talk to you or to share time with you—and who empathizes with what you are going through. By definition, a friend is someone to whom you are not related by birth or marriage, and so platonic friendships differ from the connection you feel to your siblings, cousins, parents, or even your spouse. Even a casual friend is someone who has an interest in you, someone who is more than being friendly because she or he happens to be a neighbor, classmate, a coworker, or a customer.

Friendship is something that is voluntary and has to be earned. It is that voluntary nature of friendship that makes it such a valuable intimate relationship in our lives. You choose your friends and there is a power to that.

Through my friendship research over the years I discovered that, on average, most people have 1-2 best friends and 4-6 close friends. In the "old days"—BF or Before Facebook—a network of 10-20 casual friends was typical. But as social media took hold, the number of casual friends increased dramatically. This was first revealed to me through the responses of a group of seventeen Japanese college students who in 2007 independently filled out the friendship survey that I had posted at my website. Although for seven the number of their casual friends was between four and twenty, four stated they had 50 casual friends, two had 60, one had 100, and four had 200 casual friends.

Over the years, that increased number of casual friends seems to be more common. Recently, when I visited the statistics page of Facebook, it was revealed that there are more than 800 million active Facebook users internationally; the average Facebook participant has 130 "friends." But of course that opens up the controversial debate over whether these 130 Facebook friends are friends in the way that we usually define a friend or merely acquaintances.

In fact Facebook has so altered the use of the word *friend* that I suggest that we now need a fourth category of friends, to distinguish them from tried and true friends. Just as the term BFF —best friends forever —has become popular as well as the opposite term, *frenemy*, which refers to someone who used to be a friend who is now an enemy, I propose the term FBF—Facebook "friends"—to distinguish those friends from tried-and-true friends although it is complicated because someone might have one or more best friends, one or two of their close friends, and even many of their casual friends, plus a whole bunch of strangers or fans who are now collectively this diverse group known as this new entity, FBF (Facebook friends).

Types of friends: *Dyad*, *Triad*, and Network Friendships

Beyond the level of intimacy, however, friendship tends to be categorized by how many there are in the friendship group. The typical two-person friendship, also known as a *dyad*, has a unique fragility since it takes two to start it, and maintain it, but only one to end it. The dyad is potentially the most intimate of friendships since the information that is shared, as well as the relationship itself, is between just two persons.

By contrast, the three-way friendship, or the *triad*, is somewhat easier to maintain because the friends now have another friend in common who ideally connects them but it may also not be as intimate as the two-way friendship since each three-way friendship is really only a two-way friendship, plus one. Who maintains the strongest two-way bond may shift.

The information shared in a three-way friendship may also be less exclusive or confidential than that in a two-person friendship.

Groups of friends, or networks, which include four or more friends, are again a trade-off: in general, there is less intimacy between each of the friends but more possibilities for keeping the friendships going as the interconnections expand.

It is the group of four friends that is especially idealized by the media; the American TV sitcoms that gained international fan bases, such as *Sex in the City* with its four female friends, or *Seinfeld* with its three male and one female single friends, attest to this as well as, of course, another old standby, *Friends*. The longevity of those TV sitcoms, including their popularity in reruns after their decade-long original run ended, emphasizes the benefits of a friendship group: the number of interactions between each or all of the friends is almost endless and the charm and intrigue with each friendship group, or the dyad or triad within that group, emphasizes how distinct each of the friends are from each other.

Why Friendship Affirmations and Why This Book?

I have been studying and writing about friendship for more than three decades, and doing friendship coaching for a decade, so it is no coincidence that I find this type of relationship worthy of its own collection of affirmations. This is now my fourth book of affirmations. The first one, on creative weight management, was published in 2002. The second and third books, on time management and on happiness, were released in 2011. The feedback I have received to each of those affirmations books, as well as the positive impact researching and writing these affirmations has had on my own attitudes and life, encouraged me to address friendship in this way.

The affirmations in this book are based on the original research and background readings on friendship that I have been doing over the years, starting with my 1983 sociology dissertation on friendship. I have also included around two dozen famous quotes on friendship; and, you will find a place to write down your own friendship affirmations as well as exercises or activities to do that may enhance your friendships at work or in your personal life.

As you probably know, an affirmation is a positive statement in the present tense that helps to ground our thinking and shape our behavior in a pro-active way. Two key components of affirmations are that the statements are written in a positive way and that the focus is on "now" rather than the past or the future.

Since this book is designed to enable you to read one affirmation a day, or more affirmations on a more frequent basis, if you are so inclined, you will be reinforcing a concern for friendship in your life on a regular basis. You will also be repeating some familiar and learning some fresh statements about friendship, all cast in a positive light. (For an enhanced discussion of the benefits of affirmations and related positive psychology, see the introduction to my book, *365 Daily Affirmations for Happiness*.)

The first affirmation about friendship in this book states: "I am worthy of a positive friendship." On the surface, it may seem like a simple declaration, but it is far from easy for some people to feel that way, and to say it. What if you had an abusive childhood and your parents or siblings treated you in a negative way? You might be inclined to repeat those patterns, however negative, in your friendship choices.

What if someone betrayed you when you were eleven and that made you fearful of ever again having a best friend, choosing to remain friendless rather than believing that you deserve to have a positive friendship even if that one friendship was the opposite?

Believing "I am worthy of a positive friendship" reinforces that you deserve to have such a friendship in your life. It will make it that much easier to identify and reevaluate the "pull" you may have felt since childhood toward negative people or destructive friendships or to have the courage to try again even if one or more friends have disappointed you.

Or consider the tenth affirmation: "I cut my friends some slack if they are too busy to get together, and patiently wait until it works out for their schedule." Again, this affirmation is reinforcing a constructive mindset — being patient with your friends rather than being too demanding — helping you to maintain positive friendships because you are as understanding a friend as your friends are to you.

Research in the workplace discovered that just observing workers impacted on their behavior; in the same way, just by focusing on the topic of friendship, or on a specific friend, through these positive affirmations, and doing some or all of the exercises found in this book, you are helping to improve the friendship factor in your work and in your personal life.

Every Type of Close Relationship Matters

As a friendship expert, coach, and sociologist, I am often asked which intimate relationship is more pivotal than the others: parent-child, romantic, sibling, coworkers, or friends. Fortunately, it's okay to say that each one is vital in its own way. But for those whose parents have passed away, or who do not have siblings, spouses or children, then friendship might be the most crucial close relationship in their lives, providing them with a continuity of intimacy over the years, helping them to feel connected and valued.

Even so, it is the wise friend who avoids putting her friends in the position of having to "choose" between friendship and children or grandchildren, or a friend and a spouse, for few can be in two places at once, whether physically or emotionally.

It is possible to love many, including our various friends, and to somehow find a way for everyone to feel special and cared for, even if everyone has to find a way to share you (and you have to find a way to share your friends with those they care about).

Few would disagree that it usually takes a concerted effort to stay connected to our friends. Even with the miracle of technology enabling everyone to communicate via the Internet, mobile or smart phones, as well as through social networking sites, getting together in person, or saying hello and chatting over the phone so you can hear each other's voices, takes time, energy, resources, and planning especially if you live miles away or in different time zones.

You will probably bump into your cousins at a family function that you are both likely to attend, like a wedding or a wake or funeral, but when will you see your friend again, the friend who is connected to only you? The friend who used to live next door but you are now both far away from each other, or whom you roomed with at boarding school, or knew from camp or college?

Unless you now live or work together, you will need to make specific plans to include each other in your busy lives. For those who are balancing career, education, family, romantic, or community responsibilities, making time for your friends has to still be a priority or, before you know it, you and your friends will find yourselves feeling distant from each other, an uncomfortable state to be in when you were once so close.

But if you and your friend still truly enjoy being with each other, it will of course not be a sacrifice to make the time to get together. It is a responsibility that you welcome as you nurture the caring bond that only exists because you and each of your friends chose to create your friendship, to cultivate it and now, you both want to continue it.

Ironically, because friendship is a relationship of choice, and a connection upon which few, if any, financial, physical, or legal demands are placed, it is usually one of the easiest intimate relationships to maintain and, as the research highlighted below shows, a key one to have for physical and mental health and well-being and even longevity itself.

The Benefits of Friends

Friends expand our horizons by offering us as close a glimpse at someone else's life, values, or culture as we can get beyond our own immediate surroundings.

By choosing, and maintaining, a friendship, whether it is for several months, years, or our entire lives, we have the ability to get outside of whatever specific world we were born into, not just physically but also in terms of culture, language, or even cuisine.

Think back to your own childhood. I am sure you have memories, like I do, of eating at your friend's home and tasting another cuisine for the first time, or listening to music, or watching TV programs, that your friend, or your friend's family enjoyed, that was new to you. My next door neighbor, Ginny, who was also my best friend, shared with me the Italian food of her parents, who had immigrated to the United States from Italy, and even the music of Italy and their Christmas and Easter customs.

I shared with her some of my favorite childhood foods: lox and bagels, pastrami, sour pickles, and Chinese cuisine.

Ginny was a genius at math; she actually grew up to become a high school math teacher. I benefited from being able to ask her questions about my own math homework all those hours in her basement throughout our elementary school years.

What friends helped you out when you were growing up? What are some of the foods, music, and cultures you learned about through your friends that you otherwise might not have experienced?

And this ability of our friends to expand our horizons continues throughout our lives. For example, in just the last three years, I developed a strong friendship with a literary agent who grew up in Brazil and who now lives in Spain. Our friendship has strengthened even though there is a twenty-five year age difference between us, and I am married for more than two decades and have two grown sons and a grandson, and she is living with her fiancé and they are just starting their family. We are connected through our mutual appreciation of each other as well as our book publishing careers.

I also have at least one best friend and half a dozen close friends in my age-group, friendships dating back decades. I am very typical as to how the friendships started in that most were initiated when we lived nearby, or attended school, worked together, or met through business.

Today there is wide awareness of the scientific research from the 1970s that was conducted in Northern California in the United States (Berkman and Syme)[1] and more recently studies by Harvard University doctors that confirm that having even one friend in whom you can confide may extend your life by as much as ten years. A ten-year study in Australia of 1,477 persons aged 70 and older by Giles, Glonek, Luszcz, and Andrews, written up in 2005, confirmed that having better social networks with friends and confidants predict survival over the following decade. Other studies have discovered that friendship can help someone to recover from a heart attack or breast cancer faster (or at all) compared to someone who is friendless.

We also have learned from a secondary analysis over the last decade by Nicholas A. Christakis, M.D., Ph.D., M.P.H. and James H. Fowler, Ph.D. of the results of the world-famous Framingham, Massachusetts health study that friends tend to mirror each other; their smoking, health, or weight challenges seem to be as contagious as their positive or negative attitudes about life. Another study, by Harvard Medical School and the University of California, summarized in the *Sydney Morning Herald* (Australia) in an article by Kate Benson entitled, "Why fat is a friendship issue,"

---

[1] All references are included in the Bibliography.

discovered that if a friend becomes obese "your chances of becoming obese go up 57 per cent."

Other well-publicized friendship studies include the findings published by sociologist Lynn Smith-Lovin in the *American Sociological Review* in June 2006, and written up by Janet Kornblum in *USA Today*, that the number of friends that Americans listed as those in whom they could confide had actually been reduced by one —from three people in 1985 to just two in 2004 and "one in four had no close confidants at all," wrote Kornblum.

I wonder, however, if that is because there was an actual decline in the number of friends in whom someone could confide, or if there was an increase in a reluctance to share confidences as the prevalence of social networking sites could dramatically multiply the consequences of sharing of a secret if it was confided to the wrong person. Another possibility: getting the word out about what "is" a genuine friend may have helped study participants to be more discerning in whom they labeled a "friend" than they had been in the past. Still another possibility: the increased time that was being spent online rather than getting together face to face with those special friends to share with had led to a decrease in closer friend connections or confidants, as discussed below.

Cyber-Friendships

In the last decade, it has become increasingly common for friendships to begin online. At some point, though, online friends usually find they need to move their cyberspace relationship to communicating by phone or meeting in person for the relationship to become more than just an online connection.

Although the benefit of starting friendships through the Internet that never expand beyond cyberspace is still questionable, there is no question that e-mail and the Internet, as well as being able to text message friends with a smart phone, help pre-existing friends to stay connected more easily than before.

Those are just some of the tools that help friends, often separated by physical distance, to avoid the "we've just grown apart" (in the emotional sense) syndrome that so many report as the reason that a friendship has faded or ended.

The Key Ingredients to a Terrific Friendship

Truly loving and accepting friends will approve of us despite our imperfections; hopefully, with our true friends, there is a spoken or unspoken ability to "agree to disagree" so it is unnecessary to "pretend" with each other the way we might have to with those who are not really friends.

Few if any of us would want a close or best friend who is a "yes" person out of fear of rocking the boat; we want our friends to allow us to express our varied points of view even if they differ.

As a close or best—another way of describing a

"great" friend—what you say can be all powerful if, for example, a friend asks what you think of a new romantic partner, or of a particular career decision.

Of course if there are dramatic reasons to discourage someone from the proposed choice, such as any known or suspected abusive or deviant behavior that is downright horrific so an individual is to be avoided at all costs, or a career choice that you have the learned wisdom to advise against, you may want to state your points of view in no uncertain terms, whatever the immediate consequences to your friendship.

But if it's just a question of "taste" or subjective opinion, be careful about coming down too hard on your friend's decisions or you might find your friendship dramatically strained or even suspended or ended. ("What should you do if you find yourself in that position?" is a favorite question of the media. I suggest turning it around: "You asked what I think of so-and-so. I don't know why you're asking *me*. The more important question is, 'How do *you* feel about him?'")

Yes, honesty is key to a great friendship but tact is also a pivotal consideration.

Being responsive is another powerful and key characteristic to a terrific friendship. We all may have to wait to hear back from business contacts or work relationships but our friends—our close/ best/ true/ great friends—should be treating our phone calls, our e-mails, and even our requests to get together as a priority.

And if a friend is too tired or too busy to deal with us, that's fine, too, but it needs to be understood that it's the circumstances that are causing the delay in getting together, or being responsive, not a diminishing of concern about our friend or our friendship.

In addition to honesty and responsiveness, genuine and tried-and-true friendship needs to be based on a deep, genuine feeling of liking—even loving—each other. That can't be forced. It's got to be there and it's got to continue to be there, through thick and thin, through job losses and promotions, through life choices and other relationships, through illness, and even through good and bad decisions.

Great friendships stand the test of time, and time will test even the closest of friendships. The finding from my sociology dissertation, that "shared values" is the best predictor of longevity in a friendship—more than proximity, shared interests, or even offering each other emotional support—is a view I still maintain.

Negative Friendship Patterns

Here are several common situations/feelings that characterize a negative or destructive friendship:

- Jealousy is rampant.
- Competitiveness is excessive.
- Promises are broken.

- The relationship is unequal.

Are you currently in a friendship where one or all of those situations are happening? Is this a new or transitional development, possibly related to your friend going through a rough patch because of a job loss or a romantic relationship that might be just starting or ending?

I'm not talking about whether you or your friend seem to be the one who does most of the calling on the phone, or who is more likely to send the most e-mails. There are, in most intimate relationships, those who like to do one type of activity over the other. In romantic relationships, for example, you might find one partner who does the dishes and the other makes the dinner, or one who takes care of the bills and the other one takes out the garbage. The division of labor, if you will.

In a negative friendship, it's a question of feeling that things are unequal on a much deeper level than who is making the phone calls or deciding when to get together or what movie to go see. It is the feeling that one friend is giving more to the friendship than the other is giving. It is that emotional inequality that is so very painful and a potential "deal breaker" or friendship ender.

But why do so many remain in such painful friendships? From my perspective as someone who has been studying friendship, I can say that having a lifelong friendship has become for so many—too many—the new myth that has replaced the dream of a lifelong marriage.

Yes, positive, good marriages should last a lifetime but negative or destructive intimate relationships of any kind—romantic or platonic—need to be reevaluated and possibly ended if that seems the best course of action. It is not a character flaw to realize that a friendship is negative or toxic and that it needs to at least be put on the back burner if not ended.

When should you end a toxic friendship? For each relationship, the answer will be different but, in general, you will most likely want to end a toxic friendship when it is taking a toll on your self-esteem, mental health, and, in extreme cases, your physical health or putting you or your family members in jeopardy.

Some negative friends are so negative that they put you or your other friends, family members, romantic partners, or even your career, in "harm's way," such as:[2]

- The Promise Breaker
- The Double-Crosser
- The Cheat
- The Rival
- The Abuser
- The Interloper

---

[2] For a full discussion about these and many other negative and positive types of friendships, reference my book *When Friendship Hurts,* cited in the Bibliography.

What are some other signs that a friendship is toxic? When your friend calls, you don't want to take the call, or you find yourself canceling plans to get together over and over again. Even worse, this friend is causing you such a stress reaction to her phone call, e-mails, or presence that it is making you physically ill.

If any of those situations are occurring, consider the pros and cons of winding down, or ending, your friendship or at least whether or not it is time to tactfully deal with any conflicts with your friend if you do want to try to resolve things and keep your friendship going.

How Can We Enrich Our Existing, Positive Friendships?

The very first step in improving your friendships, or even to starting a new friendship, is to make sure that you are befriending yourself. As I write in affirmation #38: "The first friend I need is myself." If you like yourself you will be more likely to be able to like others and to give to others; you will be more likely to be more accepting of the nurturing that they give back to you.

Liking, and even celebrating, oneself if you are feeling down on yourself or you have a negative self-image is a worthwhile goal. Fortunately there is help available for reclaiming a friendship with yourself if you are going through hard times or even developing positive self-esteem if it was always lacking. There are therapists who specialize in working with those who need to develop the self-love that I am referring to; reading books, such as the classic *How to Be Your Own Best Friend*, that address these issues, although not a substitute for therapy, may offer some useful tips in this area.

Developing self-love and a friendship with oneself might help a depressed or distressed child, teen, or adult get through the toughest emotional times including bullying which is having such a severe impact on so many. In the most extreme cases, bullying has been linked to such severe desperation that it was blamed for a child or teen's suicide. None of these tragic cases are simple to explain or understand, of course. Director and actress Cassidy McMillan has devoted several years to producing the award-winning documentary film, "Rats & Bullies," which tells the true story of 14-year-old Canadian teen Dawn-Marie Wesley who, after being bullied and threatened with death by three girls at her high school, committed suicide. Dawn-Marie named the three girls in her suicide note, and this tragic incident and the investigation that it prompted led, for the first time in North America, to teens being brought to trial for bullying.

Affirmation #1, "I am worthy of a positive friendship," and affirmation #38, "The first friend I need is myself," might help to offset the impact of bullying or dealing with toxic friends or pseudo-friends.

The next step to enrich the friendships we have that are positive is to make friendship a priority, not a relationship that you will get around to when you find the time after all your other concerns, personal or professional. Put friendship right up there along with your romantic partner/spouse, children, extended family, career, volunteer activities, and even your legitimate need for personal time.

By making friendship a priority, you will consider how to include your friends in your busy life. For example, if you have a local friend whom you rarely get to see, and you want to do more exercise, ask your friend if you could both commit to taking a weekly exercise class together, or meet at each other's homes once a week, or even once a month, and go for a long walk, or a jog.

Next year, at the holiday time, since you both have to shop for and wrap the presents, why not consider shopping or wrapping presents together?

In the *Friendship Journal* that I created, a blank book with selected quotes from my book, *Friendshifts*, in the back there is a place to list your key friends and to note how often you get together. It is a place to make a plan for furthering your communication with each other and putting the time and effort into your key friendships so you and your friends continue to strengthen your connection throughout the year.

Making Friends in Your Adult Years

The good news is that for most, it is a myth that it is much harder or even impossible to make new friends in adulthood than in your younger years. Consider some of the benefits of being an adult that actually make it easier to start and cultivate friendships. You are independent. You don't need a parent or baby sitter to drive you to a friend's house if your friend does not live nearby, nor do you have to have your parents' or caregiver's "approval" of a friend you'd like to hang out with. (Of course not all parents intrude on their children's or teen's friendship choices, but some do.)

What makes it "seem" like it's harder to make new friends in adulthood is that once you graduate school and start working and possibly have a family, there seems to be so much less time for friendship. In the early years, friendship is as important to one's existence as going to school.

In adulthood, there are just so many competing concerns, and some careers do not offer the opportunity to have friends at work. Even the hours that someone works might make it hard to get together with friends. In my friendship coaching, I've had clients who needed help in this area. Often it's because a job required relocation and then it seems tough to find new friends in a new town, city or country because so many in the new place already have a friendship network in place. They are hesitant to let someone new "in."

That's when it's important to think about the friendship skills that helped you out when you were a child or a teen. The skills that are necessary for forming a new friendship don't change whether you're four, ten, twenty, twenty-five, fifty, sixty-five, or even ninety.

What are those skills? First of all, you don't want to seem desperate. It's those who seem to be self-sufficient and to already have friends—who are perceived as popular—who are more likely to get more friends.

So if you are lonely and feeling desperate, instead of emotionally "pouncing" on someone new who might become a friend, continue to connect to the friends you had in your previous community, neighborhood, or job. Don't overly rely on your old friends so that you don't have the motivation to find new, more convenient friends who are sharing your new life experiences, but at least you won't have the sense of isolation or desperation that comes from feeling completely alone.

A skill that Dale Carnegie points out in his 1936 bestseller, *How to Win Friends and Influence People* that is still relevant today is to show an interest in the other person. That is the second step in making a friend.

Next, an action you can take that will help to find and cultivate new friends, whatever your age, is to pursue your interests and to be active. You will find likeminded people and, possibly, one or more with whom you feel a kinship, so a friendship may ensue.

I have observed, however, that it may start to become harder for those seniors who begin to have health issues to make new friends although if they already have friends who care about them, they will be more likely to be there for them even when physical or mental health issues become a factor. Just as health insurance is a way to have coverage if a health problem occurs, taking the time to make friends, and keeping in touch with your friends even when you relocate, whatever your age, is a form of friendship insurance.

Moving to a new residence, or even getting a new job, whatever your age, are challenges to friendships, but by understanding the dynamics of friendship these changes need not end old ties or decrease the likelihood of developing new friends. In my research, I discovered that it takes, on average, three years from when you meet till you become tried and true friends. That doesn't mean that you don't immediately form a "fast friendship" but time and the tests of time are necessary to see if this friendship is real and not superficial or what I call a foul weather or a fair weather "pseudo-friend."

A foul weather pseudo-friend needs you to be in foul weather, to be miserable. When you're employed and popular, this "friend" turns on you. Conversely, the fair weather pseudo-friend is only there for you when things are going well. Have a tough time and this friend is gonzo!

Are You a Good Friend?

In all the years I have been researching, coaching, writing and speaking about friendship, I can count on one hand the number of times someone asked me if they've been a good friend, or what they need to do to be a good friend. Most of the time, people are complaining about how someone disappointed them as a friend.

Here are some ways to tell that you're a good friend:

- You are tired, stressed, or very busy but you make the time to listen to your friend because she needs you to be there for her.
- Your friend annoys you but you take a deep breath, decide to "chill out" and not overreact, and make sure that you don't do or say anything to jeopardize this important friendship.
- You are the friend to your friends that you want others to be to you, but you also make sure you learn the individual differences between you and your friends so you don't make the mistake of pushing your needs or preferences on them if they have their own completely acceptable, different ways of doing things.
- One of your friends writes to you, by mail or through an e-mail, and says "You're a good friend."

The Role of Friendship: Expectations

When I was interviewed about friendship by Russ Mitchell in preparation for the CBS News *Sunday Morning Show* series on friendship, he asked what are reasonable expectations for a friend and friendship. I replied that it was an intriguing question since we do have very clear guidelines, even vows, that a husband and wife exchange when they marry, and there are also expectations for a parent's duties. I thought about it and decided that a Friendship Oath might be useful to consider and even to share with friends. Afterwards, I composed the following:

Friendship Oath[3]

By accepting the responsibility of friendship, I promise to be honest and trustworthy. I will try to work out any conflicts that we may have and will try to put the time and effort into our friendship that it requires.

I know we both have work (or school), family, and personal obligations, and we will respect each other's other relationships and commitments, but I will also be committed to this friendship. I will try to only give advice if you ask for it, unless, in my best judgment, I should volunteer it. I will also try to always be your friend, unconditionally.

I will keep your confidences. However, I will also share with you if it is my policy to never keep anything from my spouse or any other primary relationship, with whom I entrust all my secrets. I will try to remember your birthday and be there for you when times are tough and when times are grand.

---

[3] Written by Dr. Jan Yager. Excerpted, with permission, from *Who's That Sitting at My Desk?* by Jan Yager, Ph.D. (Hannacroix Creek Books, Inc., May 2004). You may reprint or share this oath as long as it is not edited or changed in anyway and credit is given to its author, Dr. Jan Yager, with a link, if possible, to my website: www.drjanyager.com.

Making time to talk, communicate by mail or e-mail, or getting together is a priority. I will celebrate your achievements even though I know a tiny bit of envy or competitiveness is normal. I will bring fun and joy to your life as much as I am able to as I cherish our past, present, and future friendship.

Ten Friends that Everyone Needs[4]

What follows is a list of the ten friends that every woman or man needs. However, it need not be ten separate people since some friend categories might overlap, such as The Realist who is also a Close Friend and a Same Sex Friend, or The Nurturer who is an Opposite-sex Casual Friend. A friend is someone you are not related to by either marriage or by birth. It is a noncompulsory relationship, not bound by legal ties, that usually does not include a sexual or romantic relationship; if it does, it has become something other than friendship. (However, there are exceptions as reflected in the popular term "friends with benefits," which refers to platonic friends who share sexual intimacy.)

---

[4] This essay is an edited and updated version of the article, "Ten Friends That Every Woman Needs," distributed by Kimberly Clark Corporation to major magazines including *Cosmopolitan* as part of my duties as a friendship and family consultant and spokesperson for KCC.

1. The Casual Friend

A casual friend is someone you like and who likes you, but the friendship is far from intimate. In contrast to acquaintances or those with whom you merely network, casual friends do know enough about each other that whether at work or in their businesses there is a connection. This is the easiest friendship to maintain because it lacks the emotional connection, or exclusivity, associated with close or best friendships. We learn a lot from our casual friends since information is often the basis for exchange in this type of friendship.

2. The Close Friend

Close friends are those in whom you can confide private thoughts or feelings without fear of repercussions because there is a mutual trust that confidences will not be shared. The key difference between a close and a best friend is that you can have several or many close friends; it is difficult, especially in the same geographical area, to have multiple "best" friends. Twenty-five-year-old Sonia offers this definition of a close friend: "If I am able to be myself and they feel comfortable to be themselves around me, no matter what the situation is, I would consider them my close friends."

3. The Best Friend

Like a close friend, only elevated to such an intimate level that this is "the" best friend that you have, this intimate a friend may be harder to maintain either in the workplace or once a woman or man marries and connects to her or his spouse as their best "friend." Married men often call their wife their only best friend but men, like women, still could benefit from having at least one best friend outside of marriage, someone who is trustworthy enough to share those innermost thoughts and dreams.

4. Same-Sex Friend

The same-sex friend helps you to validate or challenge your own perspectives and to be able to share about experiences along gender lines. Some of that sharing may even be in an unspoken way; being friends of the same sex there is usually a commonality of experience, such as issues related to childbearing, raising children, menopause, aging, fashion, physical changes such as menstruation, sexuality, and relationships.

5. Opposite Sex Friend

There are distinct benefits to male-female friendships, whatever the level of intimacy. Fortunately, it is no longer immediately assumed that the friendship has to be "something else." Since research has found that female friendships in general tend to be more intimate than male friendships, having an opposite-sex friend provides each gender with the chance to take a break from those gender-specific ways of connecting. In that way, a man is able to share more of his emotions with his female friend; a woman is able to have friendships with men without the self-disclosure or emotional intensity of her same-sex friends.

6. The Nostalgic Friend

You grew up together. Or you went to school together, grade school, high school, or college. Or you could have even worked together but you are no longer at the same company or even in the same field. But you need at least one nostalgic friend to help you have continuity in your life—to remind you of where you've been as a way of reaffirming how far you've traveled.

7. The Role Model

This is the friend who helps you go to the next level whether she's better at hair styling than you are or works harder or has somehow managed to find the right balance in her life among her career, romantic, childcare, and friendship pulls and choices. She's great at throwing a party and knowing who has a sale and when. You ask if you can tag along and that's fine because she's happy to have your company and you learn by her example.

8. The Motivator

When you're feeling defeated or overwhelmed, The Motivator brings you way up as she inspires you and motivates you to keep trying. Through his positive attitude, or her enthusiasm and "You can do it!" mindset, The Motivator is your cheerleader and your biggest fan.

9. The Realist

This friend doesn't put you down, but she does temper your enthusiasm and wild plans with some well-meaning realism. She's the one that reminds you that going blonde could be a great idea but be prepared for the upkeep. You want to go back to school and The Realist says, "Terrific! Great idea," but she might also remind you that you'll need to pay for it somehow.

10. The Nurturer

This friend is there with a tissue when you're sad, but she also offers to go with you to the doctor if you need a test, or to baby-sit for you if you have childcare issues. She doesn't just point you in the right direction for help. The Nurturer cares for you emotionally as well.

Ten Truths About Friendship

In summary, here are ten insights that may help you to start, cultivate, or maintain your friendships:

1. For most, once you open your heart and mind to the challenge, and rewards, of making new friends, you may actually find that it is easier to start, maintain, and grow friendships as you age, rather than harder. It will still take time and effort, but at least you can pursue any and all friends that you want to; you are in control of your friendship destiny.

2. Friendship is as much about chemistry and feelings as is love. That's why you have to move any friendships started online to meeting each other. You just might find you can't stand each other when you do meet. (But be cautious and exercise good judgment about meeting any strangers that you first get to know online; make sure you are in a public place and, if possible, bring along a longstanding friend, at least initially.)

3. You should be able to tell your friends anything you want—to share the truth—but you have to decide if you want to and what you will share!

4. Cut your friends some slack if they're going through tough time. Especially be kind to your longstanding friends because you can't ever replace those memories or years with newer friends.

5. Yes, birds of a feather flock together but remember that opposites attract so have friends that are diverse as well as similar to you.

6. Betrayal can mean not being there for someone emotionally so be careful what you promise: promise less, deliver more.

7. Don't make your friends choose between you and a romantic partner because in most cases, you know who she or he will probably choose.

8. There may be averages of how many friends are typical in each of the categories of best, close, or casual, but remember that *you* can have as many friends as you can handle!

9. Emotional support and shared activities count but always remember the fun factor in friendship.

10. Since shared values are still the best predictor of longevity in a friendship, take the time to find out your new potential friend's values and, with

your old friends, keep exploring each other so you know who someone is now, and not only what he or she was like when you first became friends.

• • • •

I appreciate you, my reader, and thank you for taking the time to read 365 *Daily Affirmations for Friendship*, writing your own affirmations at the end, as you make this book truly "your own," and doing the exercises in Part 2. For more friendship writings, go to: drjanyager.com/blog or whenfriendshiphurts.com/blog.

How wonderful it will be to receive your own friendship stories, as well as your comments about this book and its friendship affirmations. I welcome hearing from you even if a personal reply cannot be guaranteed. Send an e-mail to: yagerinquiries2@aol.com or write to: 1127 High Ridge Road, #110, Stamford, CT 06905 USA.

Happy reading, and here's to joyous friendships, always!

Dr. Jan Yager

PART I

365 DAILY AFFIRMATIONS
For Friendship

1

I am worthy of a positive friendship.

• • • •

2

I like and love myself.

• • • •

3

Physical distance is much easier to overcome between true friends than emotional distance.

• • • •

4

I put the time and energy into friendship that any worthwhile intimate relationship requires.

• • • •

5

I value friendship and I appreciate my friends. I show my friends that each one counts.

• • • •

6

I let my friends know that they are important to me.

• • • •

7

I am realistic in my demands on my friends.

• • • •

8

I know that friendship should be reciprocal so I try to give as much as I get from each friendship.

• • • •

9

I make time for my friends and I am grateful when my friends make time for me.

● ● ● ●

10

I cut my friends some slack if they are too busy to get together, and patiently wait until it works out for their schedule.

● ● ● ●

11

My friends make me feel loved and whole.

● ● ● ●

12

I know that *friendshifts* occur and that's okay. It still makes whatever friendship we have and had valuable even if it is not as close or as intimate as it once was.

● ● ● ●

13

I can handle as many friends as I want in my life, and I know that I can make time for and care about my many friends without jeopardizing any of my other personal or work relationships or responsibilities.

● ● ● ●

14

I am honest.

● ● ● ●

15

I am trustworthy.

● ● ● ●

16

I am loyal and devoted.

● ● ● ●

17

If a friend shares a secret with me, I will keep my friend's secret as long it does not compromise me in any way.

● ● ● ●

18

Every day, there are potential new friends with whom I might meet and connect. The world is full of friendship possibilities.

● ● ● ●

19

I have skills that I share with my friends.

● ● ● ●

20

"What can I do to make your life more joyful?" I may ask my friends or, if I do not use the words, I will ask myself that question and offer my help and support.

● ● ● ●

21

I am open to having casual, close, or best friends.

● ● ● ●

22

It is a privilege to be someone's friend, an honor that I take seriously.

● ● ● ●

23

I know that friendship is freely given and I am open to receiving friendship from others.

● ● ● ●

24

No matter what my balance is in the bank, I am rich because I have even one good friend.

● ● ● ●

25

Friendship is a relationship based on choice and nothing else. It is that choice that makes the relationship of friendship such a powerful one.

• • • •

26

I remember my friends' birthdays in whatever way I can but it is the concern that counts.

• • • •

27

I am there for my friends even when times are tough.

• • • •

28

I am there for my friends even when times seem easy.

• • • •

29

My cat is a four-legged friend whom I cherish.

• • • •

30

My dog is a faithful friend.

• • • •

31

If my friend needs a place to stay, I take in my friend as long as it is feasible to do so.

• • • •

32

If my friend needs money, I loan my friend money if I can afford to without expecting my friend to repay the loan until my friend is able to.

• • • •

33

Even if a friend has hurt me in the past, I forgive my friend or, if that friendship has ended, I go forward with other friends without letting that failed friendship embitter me.

● ● ● ●

34

Material goods do not substitute for friendship.

● ● ● ●

35

I love my friends regardless of their challenges.

● ● ● ●

36

I embrace the relationship called *friendship*.

● ● ● ●

37

I know that some envy or jealousy is normal in all friendships so I do not doubt those relationships just because I feel those emotions. But I do recognize when I am feeling that way and deal with it appropriately.

● ● ● ●

38

The first friend I need is myself.

● ● ● ●

39

Like the classic bestseller called *How to Be Your Own Best Friend*, I embrace that concept as I put that idea into practice every day.

● ● ● ●

40

Technology can be helpful but it
is not a friend, nor is it a foe.

● ● ● ●

41

"Thank you" are two words that I think about in regard
to my friends. I say those words to my friends.

● ● ● ●

42

"Talk soon" are two words that mean so much
when someone says it to me and I try to say it to my
friends only if I mean it because communicating
is the essence of friendship.

● ● ● ●

43

I share my feelings with my friends.

● ● ● ●

44

My friends share their feelings with me as much as they are comfortable doing so.

● ● ● ●

45

I have fun with my friends.

● ● ● ●

46

I establish traditions with my friends.

● ● ● ●

47

My friend's hopes, dreams, and fears are safe with me. I keep that information close to me.

● ● ● ●

48

"You don't need a lot of friends, just a few good ones."—Ginny Mugavero

● ● ● ●

49

"Mi casa, su casa." (My home, your home.)

● ● ● ●

50

I learn from my friends. I cherish those lessons.

● ● ● ●

51

My friends learn from me.

● ● ● ●

52

Friendship has different meanings in various cultures and I respect those similarities and disparities.

• • • •

53

Listening is one of the best tools of friendship. I work on my listening skills.

• • • •

54

Keeping any promises I make to my friends is the cornerstone of a reliable friend.

• • • •

55

I am realistic about what a friend can give to me.

• • • •

56

If I say "Sorry, I'm busy" too often to a friend, I try to figure out if that excuse is covering up something else that is going on.

● ● ● ●

57

If a friendship is worth saving, I work hard to deal with any conflicts with my friend rather than end our relationship.

● ● ● ●

58

I ask and remember the key information about my friend so she or he knows that I care about the details of my friend's life.

● ● ● ●

59

When my friends have sadness, I have sadness. When my friends have joy, I have joy.

● ● ● ●

60

I know that friendship is a feeling and you cannot force it, but I also know that I can work on the skills that make me a better friend so I can be the kind of person that friends welcome more readily into their lives.

● ● ● ●

61

I am befriending me and being good to me, taking care of my mind, my body, my spirit, my self-esteem, my relationships, my physical space, and my intellectual self.

● ● ● ●

62

Even if I am close to my siblings I also need friends who are unrelated by birth.

• • • •

63

"Friendship is a virtue, or involves virtue; and also it is one of the most indispensable requirements of life." — Aristotle, Book VIII, *The Nicomachean Ethics*

• • • •

64

I am a dedicated and caring friend.

• • • •

65

I am deserving of friends who cherish and appreciate me.

• • • •

66

"We must be our own before we can be another's." — Ralph Waldo Emerson, "Friendship," Essay VI

• • • •

67

Sports are a way to learn about being part of a team, so I participate in as many team sports as I can.

• • • •

68

Being a loner does not mean that I cannot have at least one or more friends if I want to.

• • • •

69

I like to read and that makes me feel connected to the words and the characters that I am reading; that is a type of friendship but not a substitute for friendship with people.

• • • •

70

I know that tried and true friendship takes time to develop so I am patient while it is evolving.

• • • •

71

I am a wonderful person.

• • • •

72

I know that having at least one friend to confide in will extend my life; I try to have at least one friend.

• • • •

73

My friends are an extension of me, but they are also able to show me other distinct ways of seeing the world through new eyes, ears and perspectives.

• • • •

74

"Will you be my friend?" Five words as powerful in the world of friendship as the question, "Will you marry me?" is in the world of romance.

● ● ● ●

75

Friends are not mind readers; I need to share with my friends what my concerns are rather than assume that they know.

● ● ● ●

76

"I'm made up of the people I know and the friends I keep. I'd be nothing without them."—20-year-old Penn State male, quoted in *Friendshifts*

● ● ● ●

77

Be my friend and share the wonder of my life as you and I connect.

● ● ● ●

78

Attempting to force a friendship is like trying to grab on to a snowflake as it is falling from the sky.

● ● ● ●

79

If a friendship fades or ends, I allow myself to grieve for as short or as long a time period that I need to deal with my feelings about the ending.

● ● ● ●

80

I am sensitive to the needs of others and to the reality that some people do not have even one friend… yet.

● ● ● ●

81

Dwelling on friendship or wanting a friend to change in some way is not the same thing as trying to be a friend.

● ● ● ●

82

Volunteering to help others helps me to become a better friend.

● ● ● ●

83

Taking care of those who are needy helps me to appreciate myself and my friends.

● ● ● ●

84

"In the friendship I speak of, our souls mingle and blend with each other so completely that they efface the seam that joined them, and cannot find it again. If you press me to tell why I loved him, I feel that this cannot be expressed, except by answering: Because it was he, because it was I."—Montaigne, "Of Friendship," translated by Donald Frame

● ● ● ●

85

I avoid asking my friends to choose between our friendship and their romantic or parenting relationships.

● ● ● ●

86

I would like to have friends at work but that can make it complicated so I am pleased if I have positive relationships. If friendship grows out of that, I am open to it if I think I can handle the complications.

● ● ● ●

87

I am lovable. I remind myself of those traits that I have that are lovable.

● ● ● ●

88

I am likeable.

● ● ● ●

89

They say that opposites attract. I understand that if a friend is opposite from me that I will have to deal with how that makes me feel.

● ● ● ●

90

They also say that like attracts like.

● ● ● ●

91

I read about friendship so I can learn more about this complex and key relationship.

• • • •

92

I practice what I preach about friendship by being a caring, reliable friend.

• • • •

93

I try hard to ignore gossip and to avoid spreading rumors.

• • • •

94

I am the kind of person people want to be around.

• • • •

95

Friends share achievements with each other.

● ● ● ●

96

I cry.

● ● ● ●

97

I laugh.

● ● ● ●

98

I jump up and down for joy when I feel happy.

● ● ● ●

99

I sometimes feel sad and that's okay but if it lasts too long, I look for help so I can stop being sad too often.

● ● ● ●

100

Friendship is a gift that we bestow on others and hopefully they will accept our gift but sometimes, if it is the wrong person or the wrong time, that does not mean that the gift, the friendship is wrong, it just needs to be given to someone else, or to this person at another time.

● ● ● ●

101

When it comes to friendship, quality counts more than quantity.

● ● ● ●

102

I remember to compliment my friends sincerely and regularly.

● ● ● ●

103

I think about the best friend I ever had and why she was such a wonderful friend.

● ● ● ●

104

I consider the most memorable activity I've ever done with a friend and why it was so special so I can do it again.

● ● ● ●

105

Shopping with a girlfriend is a fun way to spend time with my friend. I am careful about my comments about what my friend wants to buy.

● ● ● ●

106

I cherish my friends and let them know how much I value them and our friendship.

• • • •

107

"It is not so much our friends' help that helps us as the confident knowledge that they will help us."
—Epicurus (Greek philosopher)

• • • •

108

I value my friend and our friendship and I call just to say hello; I do not wait to share only the triumphs or the upsets.

• • • •

109

I try not to rush to judgment or be excessively demanding.

• • • •

110

I know my friend has other pulls in her life. Rather than bombard her with demands or make her feel guilty if she's busy or emotionally unavailable, I cultivate other friendships that can give me what I need till my friend is more available.

● ● ● ●

111

"I'm busy" is a phrase that friends understand but we still find a way to connect, communicate, and spend time together.

● ● ● ●

112

I cherish photos of my friends and the good times we have had together but I live in the present as well.

● ● ● ●

113

"It is one of the blessings of old friends that you can afford to be stupid with them."
—Ralph Waldo Emerson

● ● ● ●

114

If our friendship is having conflict, I try to imagine the issues from my friend's point of view so I avoid a permanent rupture in our relationship.

● ● ● ●

115

Friends may just listen even if tempted to give advice and be judgmental.

● ● ● ●

116

Friends share while respecting each other's boundaries.

● ● ● ●

117

Nostalgic friends need to cut each other a lot of slack because we're irreplaceable.

• • • •

118

"Don't walk in front of me,
I may not follow.
Don't walk behind me, I may not lead.
Walk beside me,
And just be my friend."
—Albert Camus

• • • •

119

I recognize the patterns from my childhood and how those relationships impact on my present-day choices and handling of my friends.

• • • •

120

I recognize when a friend needs my attention and I try to provide it without having to be asked.

● ● ● ●

121

I am a good listener, striving to be an even better one.

● ● ● ●

122

I have fun when I get together with my friends.

● ● ● ●

123

I "agree to disagree" with my friends.

● ● ● ●

124

"All people have their fancies; some desire horses, and others dogs; and some are fond of gold, and others of honor. Now, I have no violent desire of any of these things; but I have a passion for friends; and I would rather have a good friend than the best cock or quail in the world: I would even go further, and say the best horse or dog…"
—Plato, *Lysis, or Frienehip*

● ● ● ●

125

I let my friends know that I value them and our friendship.

● ● ● ●

126

I allow a "cooling off" period to help avoid permanent ruptures in the relationship.

● ● ● ●

127

I am empathetic.

• • • •

128

I know that a close or best friend is someone I can share anything with and I decide what I want to share.

• • • •

129

"A constant friend is a thing rare and hard to find."
—Plutarch

• • • •

130

I have commonality with my friends; we have feelings, ideas, or beliefs that we share.

• • • •

131

I am aware when feelings of jealousy or envy arise, and I avoid letting them ruin my friendships.

● ● ● ●

132

If a friend has died, I stay in communication with the family and other friends so we keep her/his memory alive.

● ● ● ●

133

"Ideally, friends offer an opportunity to undo the damage done by the family in the early years by offering the love and acceptance that parents or siblings failed to provide."—*Friendshifts*

● ● ● ●

134

I take the time to interact with my friends so that I know how they are growing now, and not just what they were like when we first met and became friends.

● ● ● ●

135

Even if I may think that I know what my longstanding friends are thinking or feeling, I take the time to check out if I am right through listening to what they say or by observing their nonverbal cues.

● ● ● ●

136

I reach out to my friends because I know that being connected offsets isolation.

● ● ● ●

137

In these days of social media communication, I still take the time to reach out to connect by phone or get together in person.

● ● ● ●

138

I know that children with friends usually do better in school so I help my child to reach out to classmates or participate in activities where friendships may form.

● ● ● ●

139

I know there is a distinct and important difference between being popular and having at least one meaningful close or best friendship.

● ● ● ●

140

"My friends are my estate."
—Emily Dickinson (poet)

● ● ● ●

141

Friendship is helping me to live longer.

● ● ● ●

142

Like love, friendship requires an investment of time and effort.

● ● ● ●

143

When I am really busy, I still try to stay connected to my friends by combining my get-togethers with something I need to do, like working out or going shopping.

● ● ● ●

144

I have a master list of birthdays, anniversaries, or special days so I remember those memorable events for my friends that I value.

● ● ● ●

145

I emphasize what is similar about me and my friend.

● ● ● ●

146

I try to avoid disappointing my friends by only making promises that I plan to keep.

● ● ● ●

147

"I was angry with my friend;
I told my wrath, my wrath did end.
I was angry with my foe;
I told it not, my wrath did grow."
—William Blake, (1757-1827), poet, "A Poison Tree"

● ● ● ●

148

"They're my friends."
"I am very well aware of that. Why do
you choose such odd friends?"
"One doesn't choose friends. One acquires them. They
are as much duty as pleasure."—Fay Weldon, novelist,
Female Friends (1974)

● ● ● ●

149

I am open to the possibility of friendship in every work
or leisure activity in which I participate.

● ● ● ●

150

I cheer myself on as well as my friends through the
tough and the joyful times.

● ● ● ●

151

I must renew my friendships and not assume old friends are there for me just because of our past together.

● ● ● ●

152

I use social media to communicate with my friends, avoiding an over-reliance on it.

● ● ● ●

153

I focus on my friend and what she is sharing with me when we meet to talk.

● ● ● ●

154

"Friendship is the only cement that will ever hold the world together."—Woodrow Wilson

● ● ● ●

155

I am friend-worthy and I remind myself of that.

• • • •

156

I show my friends how much I care through my embraces, if that is pleasant to them, and my words.

• • • •

157

I allow my friends to express their anger and I express my own anger appropriately.

• • • •

158

I decide if I agree with the proverb "Lend your money and lose your friend."

• • • •

159

By befriending myself I have more to give to others.

● ● ● ●

160

Starting new friendships is no easier or harder because of one's age; it's a mindset.

● ● ● ●

161

"What could be finer than to have someone to whom you may speak as freely as to yourself? How could you derive true joy from good fortune, if you did not have someone who would rejoice in your happiness as much as you yourself?"—Cicero, "On Friendship," translated by Frank O. Copley

● ● ● ●

162

I am a friend.

● ● ● ●

163

I am reliable and responsive.

● ● ● ●

164

I have empathy.

● ● ● ●

165

I have compassion.

● ● ● ●

166

I am fun to be around. I make an effort to be jovial.

● ● ● ●

167

I share my feelings and my possessions with my friends.

● ● ● ●

168

"Anybody can sympathize with the sufferings of a friend, but it requires a very fine nature to sympathize with a friend's successes."—Oscar Wilde

● ● ● ●

169

"Friendship is always a sweet responsibility, never an opportunity."—Kahil Gibran

● ● ● ●

170

"Will you be my friend?" Just five little words that can start a lifelong relationship of caring and concern.

● ● ● ●

171

I avoid judging myself or others based on how many friends they have at any one time.

● ● ● ●

172

I am competitive with my friends but in a way that inspires and motivates rather than sabotages or negates.

● ● ● ●

173

When my friends achieve, I achieve.

● ● ● ●

174

"It is great to have friends when one is young, but indeed it is still greater when one is getting old. When we are young, friends are, like everything else, a matter of course. In the old days we know what it means to have them."—Edvard Grieg, Norwegian composer

● ● ● ●

175

When my friends hurt, I hurt.

● ● ● ●

176

I am not worrying about the eulogy I may someday be asked to share. I work on the words everyday that I say to my friends.

● ● ● ●

177

My friends relish my success and do not pull away when things are going well for me.

● ● ● ●

178

"What is a friend? A single soul in two bodies."
—Aristotle

● ● ● ●

179

Life's ups and downs are so much more bearable if shared.

● ● ● ●

180

Sometimes I need to be alone and I pull away from my friends and that's okay. They understand that need and they patiently wait for it to pass.

● ● ● ●

181

It is an honor and a privilege to be someone's friend.

● ● ● ●

182

I hear stories of how friends occasionally traumatize each other and I try to avoid ever doing that to others.

● ● ● ●

183

I love my friends even when they annoy me.

● ● ● ●

184

"Have no friends not equal to yourself."—Confucius (551-479 B.C.), *The Confucian Analects*

● ● ● ●

185

Friends let their friends be themselves.

● ● ● ●

186

I am powerful.

● ● ● ●

187

I am mysterious.

● ● ● ●

188

Friendship is fundamental to a full and meaningful life.

● ● ● ●

189

I am kind to my friends.

● ● ● ●

190

My friends are kind to me.

● ● ● ●

191

I am a loyal friend.

● ● ● ●

192

If there was a service for "find a friend" I would be open minded about it because friends could be waiting to find other friends anywhere.

• • • •

193

I am an upbeat person.

• • • •

194

I have helpful friendships.

• • • •

195

I say "yes" to friendship.

• • • •

196

I say "no" to isolation.

• • • •

197

I embrace social media to connect with my friends but not as a substitute for a smile, a hug, an embrace, a slap on the back.

• • • •

198

I call to say, "How are you? What's new?"

• • • •

199

I call to say, "I care."

• • • •

200

"We should exercise such care in making friends that we would never offer affection to someone whom we might someday come to hate."
—Cicero, "On Friendship,"
translated by Frank O. Copley

● ● ● ●

201

I write down the names of my friends and I think about how I can be a better friend to each and every one of them.

● ● ● ●

202

I allow my friends to set their own comfortable pace to our friendship.

● ● ● ●

203

I accept feedback in the constructive
way that it is intended.

● ● ● ●

204

I am a caring, loving person.

● ● ● ●

205

I focus on what's similar about me and my friends
rather than emphasizing our differences.

● ● ● ●

206

I have body language that invites others
to want to befriend me.

● ● ● ●

207

I am open to new ideas and new people.

• • • •

208

I care.

• • • •

209

I remember.

• • • •

210

I forgive.

• • • •

211

Social media is a tool for connecting with my friends and family if I choose to use it in that way.

• • • •

212

I am a devoted friend.

• • • •

213

"Friends have all things in common."—Plato (c. 428-348 B.C.), *Dialogues, Phaedrus*

• • • •

214

I am a positive person.

• • • •

215

I know my limitations.

• • • •

216

I meditate.

• • • •

217

I cherish my friends and care about what they care about—their loved ones, their work, their favorite charities and causes.

• • • •

218

I feel good contributing to the joy of others.

• • • •

219

I take responsibility for my actions and apologize if I have done something to upset my friend.

● ● ● ●

220

My friends and I accept that occasional conflict is part of friendship and we deal with it appropriately.

● ● ● ●

221

I accept that there may be cultural differences between friends.

● ● ● ●

222

I respect my friend's choices.

● ● ● ●

223

I take the time to keep up with what's happening in my friend's life because I care about my friend.

● ● ● ●

224

I am a complex person at times and that is okay.

● ● ● ●

225

I return anything that I borrow from my friends.

● ● ● ●

226

I am curious about life. Every day is an opportunity to learn, to grow, to experience.

● ● ● ●

227

I respect my friend's boundaries and need for privacy.

● ● ● ●

228

Friendship is a high priority for me.

● ● ● ●

229

I am a pleasant conversationalist.

● ● ● ●

230

I am patient.

● ● ● ●

231

I avoid being an opportunist or using
my friends for anything.

● ● ● ●

232

"Friendship is the only thing in the world concerning
the usefulness of which all mankind are agreed."
—Cicero

● ● ● ●

233

I take my time forming a new friendship
but once I make a commitment to a friend I work hard
to keep that bond.

● ● ● ●

234

There is room in our lives for our friends and for all the relationships that we cherish, including family, other friends, or romantic partner.

• • • •

235

I am able to handle the intimacy of genuine friendship.

• • • •

236

I attract encouraging friends.

• • • •

237

I am trying my best in this friendship.

• • • •

238

I am a lifelong learner.

• • • •

239

I avoid obsessing over failed friendships.

• • • •

240

I deserve friends. Friends have earned my affection.

• • • •

241

I put myself first and I expect my friend to do the same.

• • • •

242

I am concerned about myself without being selfish.

● ● ● ●

243

"A friend to all is a friend to none."—Aristotle

● ● ● ●

244

I am selective about whom I call my friend.

● ● ● ●

245

I am not ashamed if a friendship ends.

● ● ● ●

246

I am trying to be a better friend.

● ● ● ●

247

My life is enriched by my friends.

● ● ● ●

248

I feel my friends are my soul mates.

● ● ● ●

249

I am open and honest while still being tactful.

● ● ● ●

250

I enjoy having a friend with whom I can share my thoughts, dreams, hopes, and goals.

● ● ● ●

251

I am sensitive in a constructive way.

● ● ● ●

252

I value the other points of view that my friends expose me to.

● ● ● ●

253

I allow a friendship to evolve at a pace that is comfortable for me and my new friend.

● ● ● ●

254

I am careful to avoid embarrassing my friend.

● ● ● ●

255

I give my friend the benefit of the doubt when we have issues to deal with.

● ● ● ●

256

I reread my e-mails to my friends, before I hit "send" especially if I am tired or upset, because I know that words are actions.

● ● ● ●

257

I avoid forcing feelings or relationships and let it evolve naturally.

● ● ● ●

258

I am open to new connections.

• • • •

259

I like my friends.

• • • •

260

I accept I am imperfect.

• • • •

261

I have the ability to empathize with my friends.

• • • •

262

I am trusting.

••••

263

I have high self-esteem.

••••

264

My positive, healthy friendships contribute to my excellent self-image and noteworthy self-worth.

••••

265

When I share my accomplishments, or my friends communicate their triumphs with me, I do not see that as bragging.

••••

266

"How are you?" are three little words that have so much meaning when asked of a friend.

• • • •

267

I care about my friends, and I make an effort to let them know.

• • • •

268

My friends care about me and I remind myself of their affection.

• • • •

269

Every day I remind myself of all the positive people in my life.

• • • •

270

I take the time to help those who are less fortunate.

● ● ● ●

271

I am contributing joy and meaning to my friends' lives.

● ● ● ●

272

I avoid holding a grudge. If I feel resentment, I try to work it out, within myself or with the person with whom I feel the resentment.

● ● ● ●

273

I remember the good times. I accept the bad times.

● ● ● ●

274

I am there for my friends through the bad times.

• • • •

275

Friendship is a present that is bestowed on me and that I give to others and I hold it dearer than any material goods.

• • • •

276

My friends make me smile.

• • • •

277

I deal with my friend's silence as a sign that something is going on in her life that may have little to do with me so I try to find out what is going on without jumping to any conclusions.

• • • •

278

I read to expand my world and to share my knowledge with my friends.

• • • •

279

I seek out friends in other cultures so I can gain a broader view of other people around the world.

• • • •

280

I recognize that some jealousy is normal in most friendships but I try to recognize it, and deal with it, rather than foster it.

• • • •

281

I am me and that is a great thing to be!

• • • •

282

I am aging along with my friends and it is an inevitable process that we can help each other with.

● ● ● ●

283

"How can I help?" is a genuine offer to my friends.

● ● ● ●

284

I have as many friends as I can handle emotionally and in terms of time.

● ● ● ●

285

I return phone calls, or answer a text message, from my friend as if he or she is the most important person in the world.

● ● ● ●

286

My friends and I motivate each other.

● ● ● ●

287

Today is a special day because every day is special.

● ● ● ●

288

I learn about the values that my friends have because I know that shared values are one of the best predictors of longevity in a friendship. If we have disparate values, I try to emphasize the similar ones and avoid dwelling on our differences.

● ● ● ●

289

Being a good friend is an art.

● ● ● ●

290

The passage of time is so much sweeter
because of my friends.

• • • •

291

I see any conflicts with a friend from my friend's
point of view and understand that we have unique
approaches to situations and people
because we are individuals.

• • • •

292

I am gracious.

• • • •

293

I am generous.

• • • •

294

I make the time to exercise and eat well and if possible I break bread and engage in physical activity with my friends because these are positive activities that also bond us as friends.

• • • •

295

I learn about my friend's childhood so I can understand my friend's roots better.

• • • •

296

My friendships are a high priority although I have many relationships, community, and work pulls on my time.

• • • •

297

I share activities with my friends.

• • • •

298

I see myself as an equal to my friends.

● ● ● ●

299

I am careful not to betray my friends.

● ● ● ●

300

I forgive myself for ending a friendship.

● ● ● ●

301

I forgive any friends who end our friendship.

● ● ● ●

302

I write down my thoughts about a friend if
I have issues I need to work through.

● ● ● ●

303

I am gentle.

● ● ● ●

304

I use respectful names for others.

● ● ● ●

305

I see "being busy" as a symptom that my life needs
more balance.

● ● ● ●

306

If I see myself growing apart from a friend, I try to reverse that trend.

• • • •

307

I take photos of my friends. Remembering my friends and our friendship gives continuity to our lives.

• • • •

308

I share photos of my friends with my friends.

• • • •

309

I remember my friends at the holiday time.

• • • •

310

I remember my friends all year round.

• • • •

311

If a friend moves away, I avoid standing on ceremony about who calls or visits whom to keep connected.

• • • •

312

I avoid gossiping about any failed friendships.

• • • •

313

I avoid badmouthing my current or past friends.

• • • •

314

I seek out optimistic and upbeat people.

● ● ● ●

315

I welcome a cooling off period if my friend and I disagree rather than end the friendship abruptly.

● ● ● ●

316

I recognize if a friendship needs attention and I give the time to it.

● ● ● ●

317

I validate my friends and our friendship.

● ● ● ●

318

It is powerful to affirm that I value my friends.

● ● ● ●

319

I am a valuable friend.

● ● ● ●

320

I am appreciative of each friendship I have.

● ● ● ●

321

I work at being an optimistic friend.

● ● ● ●

322

I can be the friend I have always wanted to be.

● ● ● ●

323

I can find a new friend.

● ● ● ●

324

I can improve my friendships.

● ● ● ●

325

Friends are finding me everywhere I turn and look.

● ● ● ●

326

I have a lot of friends.

• • • •

327

I have a lot to offer my friends.

• • • •

328

I am successful at finding new friends and cultivating those relationships.

• • • •

329

I have wonderful girlfriends.

• • • •

330

I have caring male friends.

• • • •

331

Every day I consider how I can let more friends into my world.

• • • •

332

I study friendship and how to be a better friend.

• • • •

333

I read about friends and relationships.

• • • •

334

I try to walk in the shoes of my friends.

● ● ● ●

335

I am independent.

● ● ● ●

336

I am a good listener.

● ● ● ●

337

I explore all kinds of friendship groups—between two, among three, or four, or more.

● ● ● ●

338

I pick up the phone, or Skype, so my friend and I speak with each other regularly.

• • • •

339

I avoid a score card with my friends and know that friendship is give and take.

• • • •

340

I include my friends whenever I can.

• • • •

341

I get professional help if I need it rather than misuse my friends as therapists.

• • • •

342

I practice giving and receiving feedback so I avoid being overly sensitive to criticism.

● ● ● ●

343

I am satisfied.

● ● ● ●

344

I am friendly.

● ● ● ●

345

I give my friends the right to choose other friends besides me or instead of me without negating the quality time we used to have.

● ● ● ●

346

I admire my friends.

• • • •

347

"A friend is a person with whom I may be sincere. Before him I may think aloud."—Ralph Waldo Emerson

• • • •

348

I share myself with my friends.

• • • •

349

I consider how to better handle conflicts that may arise between me and my friends.

• • • •

350

I avoid overreacting to a disagreement with my friend.

● ● ● ●

351

I am happy.

● ● ● ●

352

I am healthy.

● ● ● ●

353

I am productive.

● ● ● ●

354

I am an excellent friend.

• • • •

355

I have many friends in my life.

• • • •

356

I allow love to envelope me.

• • • •

357

I affirm my friend's worthiness.

• • • •

358

"The only reward of virtue is virtue; the only way to have a friend is to be one."—Ralph Waldo Emerson

● ● ● ●

359

I I accept that my friends are imperfect.

● ● ● ●

360

I am finding more friends each day.

● ● ● ●

361

I try to get the chip off my shoulder that might push my friends away.

● ● ● ●

362

I avoid throwing negative thoughts on to
the joy of my friends.

● ● ● ●

363

I am understanding when my friends have other
people, other things on their minds besides me.

● ● ● ●

364

I let my friends know that I value them. I see friendship
as a process that is constantly evolving.

● ● ● ●

365

I embrace travel as an opportunity to reconnect with old friends and to meet new ones.

• • • •

Photo credit: Jan Yager

Use the space below to record your own friendship affirmations:

366

_____

367

_____

368

369

370

371

372

373

374

375

PART II

FRIENDSHIP
Activities

At Work

1. Check off any statements below that you agree with:

    ☐ Work and friendship do not mix.
    ☐ I have at least one friend at work with whom I could have lunch or dinner or just share with about how my day is going.
    ☐ I am afraid that a work friend might find out things about me that he or she would use against me.
    ☐ I would like to have a friend at work but I don't have time for it.
    ☐ I work alone so there is no one at work to befriend.
    ☐ I value friendship at work.

    Study your answers. What have you learned about your work and friendship attitudes that might help you to approach work connections differently?

2. Consider the most positive work friendship you ever had. Who was that person? Why do you think that friendship evolved and was so positive?

    _____

    _____

3. Are you shy about initiating a work friendship? If you answered "yes," is there anything you can do to

overcome your shyness that might help you to seek out friendship at work or in your career? Joining a self-help group? Working with a social worker, therapist, psychologist, or psychiatrist? Going to a workshop? Seeking out a friendship coach?

4. Do you have anyone at work that you like to go to lunch with? If you do, make an effort to pick a specific time and date for getting together. If you lack a workplace friend, consider those with whom you interact on a regular basis. Is there anyone who has indicated that he or she wants to be your friend? If yes, what can you do to cultivate your friendship?

5. Getting together regularly as a department can help to foster friendship at work or, if you belong to an association, at a meeting. Do you have an annual or semi-annual corporate retreat or annual conference? Do you have a department or company-wide sports team? Consider founding or joining an existing group or team to encourage sharing activities beyond the work environment.

6. If you are self-employed or an entrepreneur and you work alone, do you make the time to cultivate friendships in your profession by joining, and being active in, associations or other professional activities? Do you go to conferences or training sessions that would be attended by those in your profession to develop new friendships?

   Use the space below to plan your professional membership activities for the next year that might help you to develop or strengthen business friendships:

_____

_____

_____

7. Here are some of the benefits of having a friendship at work or in business. Read over this list and add anything that is missing.
   - Work friendship can make you more productive.
   - A work friend can act as work that needs to be handled immediately.
   - A work friend will "have your back" so you will not feel as alone at work.
   - Work friends keep each other informed of trends in your company or in your profession.

Other _____

Other _____

Remind yourself of these benefits if you question the value of putting time into your work friendships.

8. Consider your work day or work week and even the way that your outside office is set up. Is there a way you might rearrange the furniture, or the work space, to foster communication, which might lead to friendships, such as a library or reading room where you could go on a break, or a break room for having your lunch, instead of eating at your desk? If you work at home or alone, are there shared work spaces that you could utilize if isolation is making it harder for you to feel positive about your typical workday? Are there

ways you might partner with others so you interact as a team and, hopefully, a work friendship might ensue?

At Leisure

1. Consider creating a friendship group and having weekly, monthly, semi-monthly, semi-annual, or annual meetings or get-togethers. It could be a discussion group, you could bring in outside speakers, or it could be related to a skill or task that you all want to explore, such as cooking or reading or writing books.

2. Make a list of your close or best friends and note how often you see each other as well as how often you communicate and by what means.

    Name

    When do you get together?

    How often do you communicate? By what means?

    Best

    _____

    _____

    _____

    _____

Close

_____
_____
_____
_____

Look over your answers. Is there a pattern to how often you get together with one, some, or all your friends? How much do you rely on social media, such as Facebook or Twitter, for communicating with your friends? How often do you communicate directly, through e-mail, the phone, or by Skype?

Do you need to put more time into face-to-face connecting with your friends? If yes, how and when will you do that?

Do you need to vary the way you communicate with your friends in-between get-togethers?

3. When is the last time you developed a new friendship? It could be a close, best, or casual friendship.

_____

If you have not developed a new friendship recently, think about what is holding you back?

What are you going to do about continuing to expand the friends in your life?

4. When was the last time you were angry with a friend?

_____

How did you handle it?

_____

If you handled it in a way that was less than satisfying, what are some other ways for dealing with conflict that you might try the next time you have a conflict with a friend?

Here is a list of nine ways of dealing with conflict from my book, *When Friendship Hurts*, so you can try to salvage a friendship. For more detailed descriptions and discussion, reference Chapter 5, "Can This Friendship Be Saved?"

- The IBB model (interest-based bargaining model) (learning to look behind problems to the reasons they happened).
- Putting yourself in someone else's shoes.
- Listening carefully and thoughtfully.
- Stepping outside the situation and taking a cinematic view.
- Agreeing to disagree.
- Validating your friendship.
- Allowing for a cooling-off period.
- Asking for understanding.
- Saying "I'm sorry" and asking for forgiveness.

If you have any other ways that you have tried, or would like to try, not included on the above list, write those suggestions down here:

_____

_____

5. Here are some friendship events that occur throughout the year on a regular basis. Consider planning activities related to each event as a way of reinforcing your friendships:

   > **May—International New Friends, Old Friends Week**
   > I founded this week in 1997 with the name National New Friends, Old Friends Week but the name was changed to "International" to recognize the impact of social media increasing the prevalence of worldwide friends. The week occurs annually in May, beginning the Sunday after Mother's Day.
   >
   > July 30—International Friendship Day
   >
   > August—National Friendship Day
   > The first Sunday in the month of August started in the U.S. in 1935 by an Act of Congress.

6. Have you considered putting together an organized friendship event that you might want to start in your community or with your friends? Connecticut radio host Mary Jones has been doing a monthly Girls Night Out in Connecticut for many years. Her sold-out events are attended by pairs or groups of friends on an occasional or regular basis.

7. Are there tasks or chores you have to do that you might want to do along with your friend? Note after each activity the names of any friends who might join you. Add any additional activities to this list if you have some possibilities that are not included.

- Shopping
- Exercising
- Volunteering or community service
- Throwing a party together
- Working on a political campaign
- Eating out
- Wrapping presents at holiday time
- Traveling
- Taking a class together
- Other _____
- Other _____

8. Do you keep a master list of your friends' birthdays and celebrate by sending a token gift, getting together, sending a card, or at least calling to mark the occasion? Keep this information in a central place so you remember each friend's special day. (You might want to check out one or both of these journals that I created: the *Birthday Tracker & Journal*, in four-color, or the black-and-white *Birthday Journal*.)

9. What is the nicest thing a friend ever did for you? that you ever did for a friend? Decide to do one nice thing for each friend without expecting any thanks or anything in return.

10. Read the Shakespearean play, "Timon of Athens," and ask yourself: were those men really Timon's friends if they stopped being his friend because he fell on hard times and could no longer treat them to luxurious dinners? Consider reading that play as a group or even

acting it out and discussing what it says about true friendship.

Bibliography

Apter, Terri and Ruthellen Josselson. *Best Friends*. NY: Three Rivers Press, 1998.

Aristotle. *Nicomachean Ethics*. D. Ross, translator. Oxford, UK: Oxford University, 1925, 1998.

Bacon, Sir Francis. "Of Friendship" (1625), in *Classic Essays in English*. Josephine Miles, editor. Boston: Little, Brown, 1965.

Barash, Susan Shapiro. *Toxic Friends*. NY: St. Martin's Press, 2009.

Baron, Gerald R. *Friendship Marketing*. Grants Pass, OR: The Oasis Press/PSI Research, 1997.

Benson, Kate. "Why fat is a friendship issue." *Sydney Morning Herald*, July 26, 2007.

Berkman, Lisa F. and Leonard Syme. "Social Networks, Host Resistance and Mortality: A Nine-Year Follow-up Study of Alameda County Residents." *American Journal of Epidemiology*, 109 (1979): 186-204.

Berry, Carmen Renee and Tamara Traeder. *Girlfriends: Invisible Bonds, Enduring Ties*. Wildcat Canyon Press, 1995.

Blieszner, Rosemary, and Rebecca G. Adams. *Adult Friendship*. Thousand Oaks, CA: Sage Publications, 1992.

Boston, Gabriella. "Keeping in touch." *The Washington Times*. November 24, 2004.

Carol, Joy. *The Fabric of Friendship*. Sorin Books, 2006.

Carnegie, Dale. *How to Win Friends and Influence People*. NY: Simon & Schuster, Pocket Books, revised edition, 1998 (1936)

Christakis, Nicolas A. and James H. Fowler. "The Spread of Obesity in a Large Social Network over 32 Years." *The New England Journal of Medicine*, Number 4, July 26, 2007, Volume 357, pages 370-379.

Cicero. *On Old Age and on Friendship*. Translated by Frank O. Copley. Ann Arbor, MI: University of Michigan Press, 1967.

De Leon, Carlos F. Mendes. "Why do friendships matter for survival?" *Journal of Epidemiology & Community Health*, volume 59, 2005, pages 538-539.

Duenwald, Mary. "Some Friends Do, Indeed, Do More Harm Than Good." *New York Times*, September 10, 2002.

Dunbar, Robin. "You've Got to Have (150) Friends," *The New York Times*, December 25, 2010.

Faller, Mary Beth. "Bronx Buddies: 7 women keep 40 year friendship flourishing." *Stamford Advocate*, August 15, 2002, pages C1, C3.

Emerson, Ralph Waldo. "Friendship," in *Essays by Ralph Waldo Emerson*. NY: Harper and Row, 1951, pages 121-156.

Frankl, Victor E. *Man's Search for Meaning*. NY: Simon & Schuster/Touchstone Books, 1984.

Gee, Lisa. *Friends: Why Men and Women are from the Same Planet*. London, UK: Bloomsbury, 2004.

Giles, Lynne C.; Gary F.V. Glonek; Mary A. Luszcz; and Gary R. Andrews. "Effect of Social networks on 10 year survival in very old Australians: the Australian longitudinal study of aging." *Journal of Epidemiology & Community Health*. Volume 59, 2005, pages 574-579.

Greive, Bradley Trevor. *Friends to the End*. Kansas City, KS: Andrews McMeel Publishing, LLC, 2004.

Griffin, Katherine. "Friends: The secret to a longer life." *Reader's Digest*, September 2002.

Haupert, Debba. *Girlfriendology 101: Simple Steps to More Fulfilling Friendships*. Seattle, WA: Kindle edition, 2011.

House, James S.; Karl R. Landis; and Debra Umberson. "Social Relationships and Health." *Science*, Volume 241, July 29, 1988, pages 540-545.

Isaacs, Florence. *Toxic Friends, True Friends*. NY: Morrow, 1997.

Kleinfield, N.R. "In Death Watch for Stranger, Becoming a Friend to the End." *The New York Times*, January 25, 2004, pages 1, 34.

Kornblum, Janet. "Study: 25% of American have no one to confide in." *USA Today*, June 23, 2006, page 01A.

Kroenke, Candyce; Laura D. Kubzansky; Eva S. Schernhammer; Michelle D. Holmes; and Ichiro Kawachi. "Social Networks, Social Support, and Survival After Breast Cancer Diagnosis." *Journal of Clinical Oncology*, Volume 24, March 1, 2006, pages 1105-1111.

Levine, Irene. *Best Friends Forever: Surviving a Breakup with Your Best Friend*. NY: Overlook Press, 2009.

Lindsey, Karen. *Friends as Family*. Boston: Beacon Press, 1981.

Luongo, Janet. *365 Daily Affirmations for Creativity*. Foreword by Jack Canfield. Stamford, CT: Hannacroix Creek Books, Inc., 2005.

McGreal, Chris. "Nine teenagers charged over bullying that led to girl's suicide." *The Guardian*, www.guardian.co.uk, March 29, 2010.

Mills, Eleanor. "Facebook's friendship trap." From *The Sunday Times*, www.timesonline.co.uk, May 30, 2010.

Newman, Mildred, Bernard Berkowitz, with Jean Owen. *How to Be Your Own Best Friend*. NY: Ballantine Books, 1986.

Montaigne, "Of Friendship." In *Complete Essays of Montaigne*, edited and translated by Donald M. Frame. Stanford, CA: Stanford University press, 1958, pages 135-144.

Olds, Dorri. "Defriending My Rapist." *New York Times*, January 15, 2012, page 3.

Orth-Gomer, K.; A. Rosengren; and L. Wilhelmsen. "Lack of social support and incidence of coronary heart disease in middle-aged Swedish men." *Psychosomatic Medicine*, volume 55, 1993, pages 37-43.

Parker-Pope, Tara. "What Are Friends For? A Longer Life." *New York Times*, April 20, 2009, page D1, New York edition.

Pausch, Randy and Jeffrey Zaslow. *The Last Lecture*. NY: Hyperion, 2008.

Plato. *Lysis or Friendship* in *The Works of Plato*, Irwin Edman, ed. NY: Modern Library, 1928.

Pryor, Liz. *What Did I Do Wrong?* NY: Free Press, 2010.

Rath, Tom. *Vital Friends*. NY: Gallup Press, 2006.

Roel, Ronald E. "Pivotal friendships." *Newsday*, March 12, 2005.
Rubin, Lillian B. *Just Friends*. NY: Harper, 1985.

Sacramento Bee. "Communicating is Easier than Ever: So Why do so Many Americans Have Fewer Close Friends?" August 6, 2006, distributed by McClatchy-Tribune Business News.

Sefton, Dru. "How Big is Your Circle of Friends?" Newhouse News, 2006.

Thoreau, Henry David. *The Portable Thoreau*. NY: Viking, 1964.

Vernon, Mark. *The Meaning of Friendship*. NY: Palgrave Macmillan, 2010.

Vora, Shivani. "A Deluxe Vacation, your Friends Included." *New York Times*, October 26, 2006.

Welty, Eudora and Ronald A. Sharp. Ed. *The Norton Book of Friendship*. NY: Norton, 1991.

Wheeler, Sheba B. "The ups and downs of letting go of relationships that have soured." *The Denver Post*, April 14, 2006.

Yager, Jan. *365 Daily Affirmations for Creative Weight Management*. Stamford, CT: Hannacroix Creek Books, Inc., 2002.

_____. *365 Daily Affirmations for Happiness*. Stamford, CT: Hannacroix Creek Books, Inc., 2011.

_____. *365 Daily Affirmations for Time Management*. Stamford, CT: Hannacroix Creek Books, Inc., 2011.

_____. *Birthday Tracker & Journal*. Stamford, CT: Hannacroix Creek Books, 2011.

_____. *Friendshifts: The Power of Friendship and How it Shapes Our Lives*. 2nd edition. Stamford, CT: Hannacroix Creek Books, Inc., 1997, 1999.

_____. "Friendship Patterns of Young Urban Single Women." (by J.L. Barkas) Dissertation, The City University of New York Graduate Center, 1983.

_____. "Perspectives on Friendship." Special issue on Sociological Practice, edited by Ray Kirshak. *International Journal of Sociology and Social Policy*. Vol. 18, No. 1. 1998, pages 27-40.

_____. *When Friendship Hurts*. NY: Simon & Schuster/Fireside Books, 2002.

Zaslow, Jeffrey. *The Girls from Ames: A Story of Women and a Forty-Year Friendship.* New York: Gotham Books, 2009.

Resources

www.whenfriendshiphurts.com
The official website for my book, *When Friendship Hurts*, as well as for related friendship topics. You can find free book excerpts as well as my blog: www.friendshiphurts.com/blog

You will find additional excerpts from my book *Friendshifts* as well as relationship writings at my main website: www.drjanyager.com and a blog on a range of topics including friendship at www.drjanyager.com/blog

http://www.friendship.com.au/
The Friendship Page
Started in 1996 by Australian Bronwyn Polson, this popular site includes a friendship chat room, quotes on friendship, as well as a highlighting of the annual International Friendship Day.

www.girlfriendology.com
Founded by Debba Haupert, includes a blog, podcast, and a community of women to discuss and connect about friendship. (If you want to hear the podcast I did on friendship for this site, go to: http://girlfriendology.com/blog/2353/girlfriendology-blogtalkradio-interviews-dr-jan-yager-friendship-expert/)

www.selfgrowth.com
Free online resource with articles, videos, and newsletters related to the areas of success, love and relationships, health and fitness, money and careers, and lifestyle.

www.thefriendshipblog.com
Blog maintained by Irene Levine, Ph.D., psychologist and author of *Best Friends Forever.*

www.thelastlecture.com
Site devoted to Randy Pausch's last lecture. Offers a link to watch "The Last Lecture" as well as an excerpt from the book of the same name (*The Last Lecture*) and biographical information on the author and co-author.

http://whatfriendsdo.com
Launched in 2007 by Aimee Kandrac and her mother Fran, an outgrowth of a site that had been developed in 2005 to coordinate information and help for her sister Stephanie's best friend Laura, who was being treating for a terminal brain tumor, this free site now helps thousands of friends-helping-friends teams. "It's the little things that friends can do in twenty minutes or half an hour that can really change your outlook and make things feel just a little bit better," says co-founder Aimee, who runs the site fulltime.

About the Author

Jan Yager is a friendship and relationship and business coach, speaker, writer, and author of 31 books translated into 30 languages. Her academic background includes a college degree with a major in fine arts, a year of graduate work in art therapy, a Masters in criminal justice, and a Ph.D. in sociology from The City University of New York. Dr. Yager has taught over the years at the college level including Penn State, St. John's University, The New School and the University of Connecticut.

Author of three other books on friendship—*Friendshifts: The Power of Friendship and how It Shapes Our Lives; When Friendship Hurts;* and *Friendship: A Selected, Annotated Bibliography*—Dr. Yager has researched friendship since the late 1970s. She has delivered keynote addresses and conducted workshops on friendship throughout the U.S. and internationally.

For more information, and to read Dr. Yager's original blogs, go to: www.drjanyager.com, whenfriendshiphurts.com, fax (203) 968-0193, e-mail: yagerinquiries2 @aol.com, or write to: Dr. Jan Yager, 1127 High Ridge Road, #110, Stamford, CT 06905 USA. Follow her tweets at: twitter.com/drjanyager.

Other Affirmation Books
Published by Hannacroix Creek Books, Inc.
www.hannacroixcreekbooks.com
(Available at your favorite online or local bookstore)

365 DAILY AFFIRMATIONS FOR CREATIVITY by Janet Luongo
Foreword by Jack Canfield (co-author, *Chicken Soup for the Soul* series) Affirmations to inspire creativity, divided into 12 categories with an additional 60 exercises for individuals and managers.
"Janet Luongo will take you on a journey of self-discovery and self-awareness that will lead you to a whole new level of creativity."
—Janet E. Lapp, RN, Ph.D., author, *Positive Spin*

365 DAILY AFFIRMATIONS FOR TIME MANAGEMENT by Jan Yager, Ph.D.
Positive statements reinforcing your productivity; includes an introduction, exercises for improving work and personal time, a bibliography, resources and index.
"Read this book for inspiration, motivation, and insights into how to improve the way you handle your time work or leisure time. I love this book! It's a gem!"
—Julie Jansen, author, *I Don't Know What I Want, But I Know It's Not This*

365 DAILY AFFIRMATIONS FOR CREATIVE WEIGHT MANAGEMENT by Jan Yager, Ph.D.
These affirmations reinforce a positive attitude toward a readers' body image and physical self, whatever their weight, including suggestions about what to do besides grabbing food out of boredom and other emotions, or just plain habit.
"Provides inspiring, practical guidance for developing healthy attitudes regarding health and weight management."
—Jeffrey R. Wilbert, Ph.D., co-author, *Fattitudes*®

365 DAILY AFFIRMATIONS FOR HAPPINESS by Jan Yager, Ph.D.
Includes an introduction that highlights of happiness research, affirmations and selected famous happiness quotes, plus activities for enhancing happiness at work and in your personal life; bibliography; and resources.
"*365 Daily Affirmations for Happiness* is an antidote to stress and busyness."—Leslie Yerkes, author, *Fun Works: Creating Places Where People Love to Work*

www.ingramcontent.com/pod-product-compliance
Lightning Source LLC
LaVergne TN
LVHW051835080426
835512LV00018B/2884